SUPER SIMPLE DIY

MAKE A SPACESHIP

YOUR WAY!

Rachael L. Thomas

Consulting Editor, Diane Craig,
M.A./Reading Specialist

Super Sandcastle

An Imprint of Abdo Publishing
abdobooks.com

abdobooks.com

Published by Abdo Publishing, a division of ABDO, PO Box 398166, Minneapolis, Minnesota 55439. Copyright © 2019 by Abdo Consulting Group, Inc. International copyrights reserved in all countries. No part of this book may be reproduced in any form without written permission from the publisher. Super SandCastle™ is a trademark and logo of Abdo Publishing.

Printed in the United States of America, North Mankato, Minnesota
102018
012019

THIS BOOK CONTAINS RECYCLED MATERIALS

Design: Sarah DeYoung, Mighty Media, Inc.
Production: Mighty Media, Inc.
Editor: Megan Borgert-Spaniol
Content Consultant: Benjamin J. Garner
Cover Photographs: iStockphoto; Shutterstock
Interior Photographs: iStockphoto; Michael Goldenkov/Strelka Institute/Flickr; Shutterstock

The following manufacturers/names appearing in this book are trademarks:
Elmer's®, Quaker®

Library of Congress Control Number: 2018948791

Publisher's Cataloging-in-Publication Data
Names: Thomas, Rachael L., author.
Title: Make a spaceship your way! / by Rachael L. Thomas.
Description: Minneapolis, Minnesota : Abdo Publishing, 2019 | Series: Super simple DIY
Identifiers: ISBN 9781532117206 (lib. bdg.) | ISBN 9781532170065 (ebook)
Subjects: LCSH: Space ships--Juvenile literature. | Handicraft--Juvenile literature. |
    Creative activities and seat work--Juvenile literature.
Classification: DDC 680--dc23

Super SandCastle™ books are created by a team of professional educators, reading specialists, and content developers around five essential components—phonemic awareness, phonics, vocabulary, text comprehension, and fluency—to assist young readers as they develop reading skills and strategies and increase their general knowledge. All books are written, reviewed, and leveled for guided reading and early reading intervention programs for use in shared, guided, and independent reading and writing activities to support a balanced approach to literacy instruction.

TO ADULT HELPERS

The projects in this book are fun and simple. There are just a few things to remember to keep kids safe. Some projects may use sharp or hot objects. Also, kids may be using messy supplies. Make sure they protect their clothes and work surfaces. Be ready to offer guidance during brainstorming and assist when necessary.

CONTENTS

BECOME A MAKER

A makerspace is like a laboratory. It's a place where ideas are formed and problems are solved. Kids like you create amazing things in makerspaces. Many makerspaces are in schools and libraries. But they can also be in kitchens, bedrooms, and backyards. Anywhere can be a makerspace when you use imagination, inspiration, **collaboration**, and problem-solving!

IMAGINATION

This takes you to new places and lets you experience new things. Anything is possible with imagination!

INSPIRATION

This is the spark that gives you an idea. Inspiration can come from almost anywhere!

MAKERSPACE TOOLBOX

COLLABORATION

Makers work together. They ask questions and get ideas from everyone around them. **Collaboration** solves problems that seem impossible.

PROBLEM-SOLVING

Things often don't go as planned when you're creating. But that's part of the fun! Find creative **solutions** to any problem that comes up. These will make your project even better.

IMAGINE A SPACESHIP

DISCOVER AND EXPLORE

Spaceships allow humans to explore what exists beyond Earth. You can learn all about real space flights in museums and on the internet. You can also explore spaceships in science **fiction**. What is your favorite kind of spaceship? What do you like about it?

GET INSPIRED!
See page 24

IMAGINE

If you could make any spaceship, what would it be like? Would your spaceship fly to the moon? Or would it zoom to a **galaxy** not yet discovered? Is it commanded by humans or a band of **aliens**? Remember, there are no rules! Let your imagination run wild!

7

BRING YOUR SPACESHIP TO LIFE

It's time to turn your dream spaceship into a makerspace marvel! What did you like most about your dream spaceship? Its rocket boosters? Its wings? How could you use the materials around you to create these features? Where would you begin?

INSPIRATION

The National Air and Space Museum in Washington, DC, holds a collection of spaceships. One is the *Columbia*, a three-person space **vehicle**. It was used in 1969 to take humans to the moon for the first time!

COLLABORATE!
See page 28

BE SAFE, BE RESPECTFUL

MAKERSPACE ETIQUETTE

THERE ARE JUST A FEW RULES TO FOLLOW WHEN YOU ARE BUILDING YOUR SPACESHIP:

1. **ASK FOR PERMISSION AND ASK FOR HELP.** Make sure an adult says it's OK to make your spaceship. Get help when using sharp tools, such as scissors, or hot tools, like a glue gun.

2. **BE NICE.** Share supplies and space with other makers.

3. **THINK IT THROUGH.** Don't give up when things don't work out exactly right. Instead, think about the problem you are having. What are some ways to solve it?

4. **CLEAN UP.** Put materials away when you are finished working. Find a safe space to store unfinished projects until next time.

GATHER YOUR MATERIALS

Every makerspace has different supplies. Gather the materials that will help you build the spaceship of your dreams!

STRUCTURE

These are the main materials you will use to build your spaceship's body.

CONNECTING

These are the materials you will use to hold your spaceship together.

COLLABORATE!
See page 28

DECORATIONS & DETAILS

These are the materials you will use to make your spaceship look cool and bring it to life!

⚠ STUCK?

LOOK BEYOND THE USUAL CRAFT SUPPLIES! THE PERFECT SHAPE MIGHT BE IN YOUR KITCHEN CABINET, GARAGE, OR TOY CHEST. SEARCH FOR MATERIALS THAT MIGHT SEEM SURPRISING.

11

BUILD YOUR SPACESHIP'S BODY

Every structure is made up of different shapes. How can you put shapes together to make your dream spaceship?

INSPIRATION

Spaceships are shaped to move through the air with ease. Find curved materials, such as bottles and cups, that will help your spaceship cut through the atmosphere.

GET INSPIRED!
See page 24

⚠ STUCK?

SPACESHIPS ARE OFTEN MADE OF METAL AND GLASS. MATERIALS SUCH AS ALUMINUM FOIL AND CLEAR PLASTIC CAN CREATE A SIMILAR LOOK. WHAT OTHER SHINY MATERIALS CAN YOU FIND?

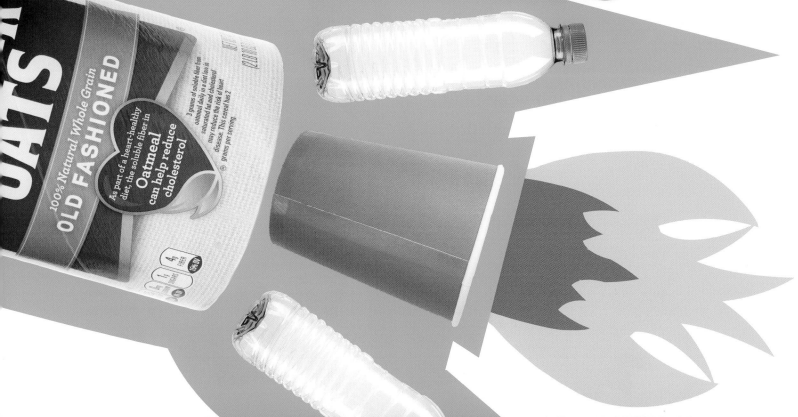

GIVE YOUR SPACESHIP A MISSION

A mission is a task or purpose. What is your spaceship's mission? Knowing this will help you figure out what materials you could use to construct your spaceship.

Will it be sending humans to Mars?

Then it will need rocket boosters and a **space shuttle** for astronauts.

DIY

Will it travel to Earth to study humans?

Then it will need a flying-saucer body and landing gear!

Your flying saucer needs an opening for pulling in Earthlings!

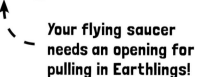

IMAGINE

WHAT IF YOUR SPACESHIP WERE A LIVING CREATURE THAT FLEW THROUGH SPACE WITH A CREW ON ITS BACK?

15

In 1975, artist Syd Mead helped **design** the science-**fiction** film *Star Trek: The Motion Picture*. Mead finished his design for the spaceship *V'ger* on a paper napkin! Mead has since worked on other science-fiction films, such as *Blade Runner* and ***Aliens***.

Will it house humans vacationing in space?

Then create features to make it fun and comfortable for space guests.

COLLABORATE!
See page 28

Will it travel through space and time?

Then use shiny materials to give your ship a **futuristic** look.

⚠ STUCK?

YOU CAN ALWAYS CHANGE YOUR MIND IN A MAKERSPACE. ARE YOU STRUGGLING TO FIND MATERIALS THAT LOOK LIKE SMOKE OR FIRE? USE THE COLORS THAT YOU CAN FIND. YOUR SPACESHIP CAN RUN ON A FUTURISTIC FUEL THAT BURNS GREEN AND PURPLE!

CONNECT YOUR SPACESHIP

Will your spaceship be **permanent**? Or will you take it apart when you are finished? Knowing this will help you decide what materials to use.

TOTALLY TEMPORARY

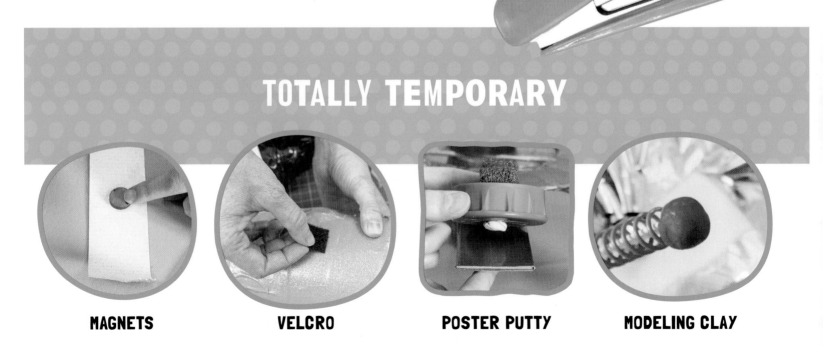

MAGNETS   VELCRO   POSTER PUTTY   MODELING CLAY

PROBLEM-SOLVE!
See page 26

IMAGINE

ANY SPACESHIP THAT VISITS ANOTHER PLANET NEEDS TO BE READY FOR LANDING! HOW WOULD YOUR SPACESHIP NEED TO ADAPT FOR LANDING ON WATER, ICE, OR EVEN HOT, LIQUID ROCK?

A LITTLE STICKY

CLEAR TAPE

STAPLES

SUPER STICKY

DUCT TAPE

HOT GLUE

DECORATE YOUR SPACESHIP

Decorating is the final step in making your spaceship. It's where you add **details** to your spaceship. How do your decorations bring your spaceship to life?

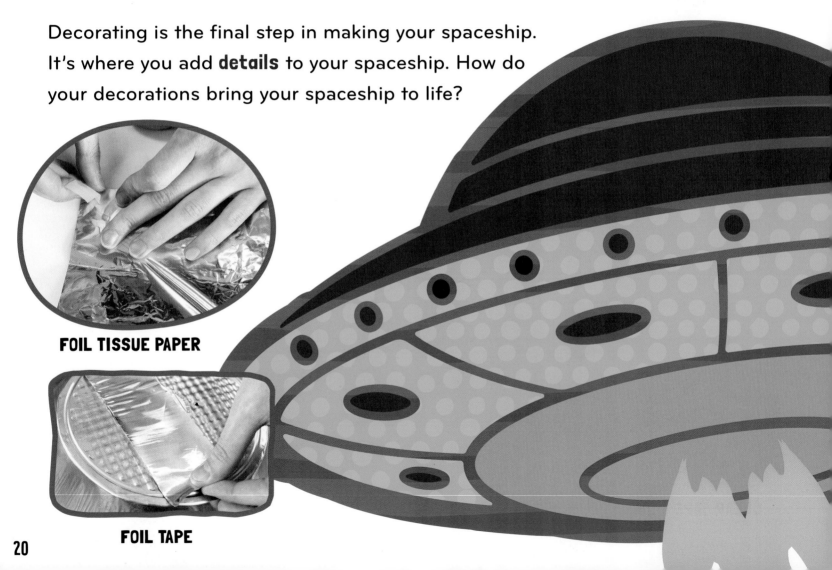

FOIL TISSUE PAPER

FOIL TAPE

GET INSPIRED!
See page 24

**BOTTLE CAPS AND
FOAM NOODLES**

DUCT TAPE

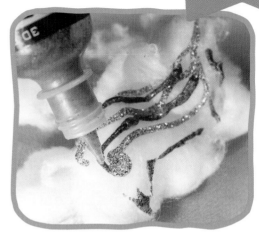

**COTTON BALLS AND
GLITTER GLUE**

SPRINGS

CORKS

IMAGINE

IS THE COMMANDER OF YOUR
SHIP GOOD OR EVIL? HOW
DOES THIS AFFECT HOW YOU
DECORATE YOUR SPACESHIP?

21

HELPFUL HACKS

As you work, you might discover ways to make challenging tasks easier. Try these simple tricks and **techniques** as you construct your spaceship!

Fix magnets under duct tape for a hidden connection.

Stick shiny tape under glass beads to make them look reflective.

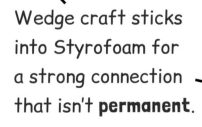

Wedge craft sticks into Styrofoam for a strong connection that isn't **permanent**.

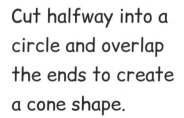

Cut halfway into a circle and overlap the ends to create a cone shape.

PROBLEM-SOLVE!
See page 26

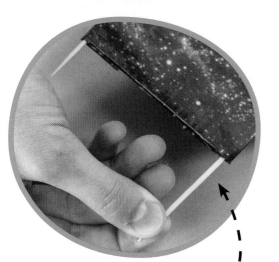

Use toothpicks to connect the window to the spaceship body.

Cut partway into cardboard with a craft knife to help it fold.

Brass fasteners allow the spaceship wings to move.

⚠ STUCK?

MAKERS AROUND THE WORLD SHARE THEIR PROJECTS ON THE INTERNET AND IN BOOKS. IF YOU HAVE A MAKERSPACE PROBLEM, THERE'S A GOOD CHANCE SOMEONE ELSE HAS ALREADY FOUND A SOLUTION. SEARCH THE INTERNET OR LIBRARY FOR HELPFUL ADVICE AS YOU MAKE YOUR PROJECTS!

GET INSPIRED

Get inspiration from the real world before you start building your spaceship!

LOOK AT REAL SPACESHIPS

Look at images of real-life spaceships. Most are sent into space using rockets. Some have a crew and living space. What other features do you notice? How can you create these features for your spaceship?

LOOK AT SPACESHIPS IN MOVIES

Hundreds of movies are set in space. Most of the spaceships in these movies were dreamed up by artists and have never been built in real life. What would your science-**fiction** spaceship look like?

LOOK AT OTHER VEHICLES

Spaceships have a lot in common with other **vehicles**, such as cars, trains, boats, and airplanes. Get inspiration from these vehicles. Which of their features can you borrow for your spaceship?

PROBLEM-SOLVE

No makerspace project goes exactly as planned. But with a little creativity, you can find a **solution** to any problem.

FIGURE OUT THE PROBLEM

Maybe your spaceship keeps tipping over. Why do you think this is happening? Thinking about what may be causing the problem can lead you to a solution!

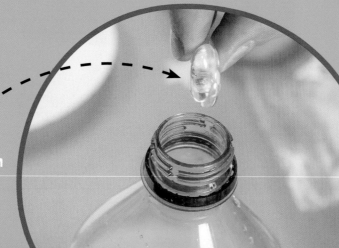

 SOLUTION: Put glass beads inside the ship's body to help weigh it down.

SOLUTION: Attach paper cups to the rocket boosters to widen their bases.

26

BRAINSTORM AND TEST

Try coming up with three possible **solutions** to any problem. Maybe your space hotel is not staying balanced and upright. You could:

1. Use heavier materials for the center of the structure.

2. Cut the spokes so they are shorter and lighter.

3. Arrange the bottle caps on the spokes so they are closer to the center.

Test all three and see which works best!

ADAPT

Still stuck? Try a different material or change the **technique** slightly.

COLLABORATE

Collaboration means working together with others. There are tons of ways to collaborate to build a spaceship!

ASK A FELLOW MAKER

Talk to a friend, classmate, or family member. Other makers can help you think through the different steps to building a spaceship. These helpers can also lend a pair of hands during construction!

ASK AN ADULT HELPER

This could be a teacher, librarian, grandparent, or any trusted adult. Describe what you want a material to do instead of asking for a specific material. Your helper might think of items you didn't know existed!

ASK AN EXPERT

An **expert** in rocket science could explain what real spaceships need to function. An artist could tell you about the process of imagining and **designing** a **fictional** spaceship!

THE WORLD IS A MAKERSPACE!

Your spaceship may look finished, but don't close your makerspace toolbox yet. Think about what would make your spaceship better. What would you do differently if you built it again? What would happen if you used different **techniques** or materials?

IMAGINATION

INSPIRATION

COLLABORATION

PROBLEM-SOLVING

DON'T STOP AT SPACESHIPS

You can use your makerspace toolbox beyond the makerspace! You might use it to accomplish everyday tasks, such as organizing a club or caring for pets. But makers use the same toolbox to do big things. One day, these tools could help govern nations or maintain public parks. Turn your world into a makerspace! What problems could you solve?

GLOSSARY

alien – a being coming from outside Earth.

collaborate – to work with others.

design – to plan how something will appear or work. A design is a sketch or outline of something that will be made.

detail – a small part of something.

expert – a person who is very knowledgeable about a certain subject.

fiction – stories that are not real.

futuristic – relating to the future, the time that hasn't happened yet.

galaxy – a very large group of stars, planets, and other objects in space.

permanent – meant to last for a very long time.

solution – an answer to, or a way to solve, a problem.

space shuttle – a spacecraft that carries people and cargo between Earth and space.

technique – a method or style in which something is done.

vehicle – a machine used to carry people or goods.